The Best Damn Management Book Ever

The Best Damn Management Book Ever

9 Keys to Creating Self-Motivating High Achievers

WARREN GRESHES

WILEY

John Wiley & Sons, Inc.

Published by John Wiley & Sons, Inc., Hoboken, New Jersey.
Published simultaneously in Canada.

For general information on our other products and services or for technical support, please contact our Customer Care Department within the United States at (800) 762-2974, outside the United States at (317) 572-3993 or fax (317) 572-4002.

Wiley publishes in a variety of print and electronic formats and by print-on-demand. Some material included with standard print versions of this book may not be included in e-books or in print-on-demand. If this book refers to media such as a CD or DVD that is not included in the version you purchased, you may download this material at http://booksupport.wiley.com. For more information about Wiley products, visit www.wiley.com.

Library of Congress Cataloging-in-Publication Data:

Greshes, Warren, 1951–
    The best damn management book ever : 9 keys to creating self-motivating
high achievers / Warren Greshes.
        p. cm.
    ISBN 978-1-118-03232-9 (hardback); ISBN 978-1-118-16131-9 (ebk);
    ISBN 978-1-118-16130-2 (ebk); ISBN 978-1-118-16050-3 (ebk)
    1. Management.   2. Motivation (Psychology)   3. Communication.   I. Title.
HD31.G7623 2011
658–dc23

                                                                    2011032041

Printed in the United States of America.

10 9 8 7 6 5 4 3 2 1

This book is dedicated to four people:

First to my dad, Arthur Greshes, who passed away two years ago. Thanks Dad, for teaching me how to be a great father. I just wish you could have lasted one more year to see the Giants win the World Series. You would have loved it.

Next, to my son Michael and daughter Emily, who have been real good sports about letting me reveal so many of their secrets within these pages. And no, you guys are not getting a cut of the royalties.

And last, but of course, not least, to my wife, Linda, the better part of me. I just don't make any sense without you.

Contents

Introduction

Anyone who knows me knows I am a maniacal sports fan. I religiously follow Major League Baseball (San Francisco Giants), NFL football (New York Giants), and NBA basketball (Boston Celtics). My knowledge of useless sports trivia has won me numerous drinks in more bars than I care to remember. I see nothing wrong with Jimmy Fallon's character in the movie *Fever Pitch*. My wife, of course, gets depressed whenever she watches it.

"What's the point?" you ask. "Isn't this a management book?" Yes, it is. The point is I have witnessed, for more than 50 years, what it takes to win a championship in professional sports, and, for the past 38 years, what it takes to manage and operate a successful business, and guess what? It's the same thing: a great management team!

What turned General Motors from the biggest and one of the best companies in the world to a bankrupt shell of its former self, standing on the government bailout line with its hand out? Bad management!

What's the difference between the Brooklyn/Los Angeles Dodgers of the 1950s, 1960s, 1970s, 1980s, and 1990s—one of the crown jewel franchises in all of Major League Baseball—and the laughing-stock of a team we see today that has had trouble meeting payroll and hasn't won a championship in 23 years? And don't think that as a Giants fan I'm not loving this.

I'll tell you the difference: the man at the top. For over 40 years the O'Malley family (father Walter and son Peter) built a model organization that prided itself on doing things "the Dodger way," from the major league team down through the minor leagues and into the front office. The man at the top now is Frank McCourt, who, together with his wife, has run the team like a corner candy store—a "Mom and Pop" business, while allegedly siphoning off money to support their lavish lifestyle. They've allegedly taken money from such departments as player development (which is used to scout for, sign, and develop young prospects into major league players), and used it to live like Marie Antoinette and Louie XVI.

What U.S. airline is consistently rated the best domestic airline in the sky? Southwest, of course. Why? Because of the vision and culture created at the top of the organization by one man: Herb Kelleher.

Inside this book you'll read stories about two managers/leaders: my first boss, Sal, one of the worst managers of all time, and my best friend, Alan Weinstock, one of the best managers I've ever seen in my business travels. The stories of these two men give you a great look at what to do and, of course, what *not* to do.

Being a manager is a tough job. You are the key link in any organization. Let's face it, if you take a great staff, put them through the finest training programs, and then send them off to work with a bad manager, you soon have a bad staff. Of course, the opposite is true, too. Take a mediocre or bad staff and hand them over to a great manager, and you soon have a terrific staff.

One of the things that make the job so difficult is the number of hats great managers must wear. There's the strategic planning hat; then there are the recruiting, hiring, and retention hats. In addition, you have the training hat, the networking hat, the motivational speaker hat, the dreaded paperwork and reporting hat. How about the "I have to deal with the home office" hat; the parent and mentor hat—and if you haven't noticed that being a people leader is a lot like being a parent, then you haven't been paying attention. Last but not least, for many managers there's the personal production hat.

Bottom line: With all the hats managers wear and all the responsibilities they have, the single biggest commodity managers have the least of is time. That's why this book, *The Best Damn*

Management Book Ever: 9 Keys to Creating Self-Motivated High Achievers, is dedicated to one thing: making you a more effective leader by teaching you how to develop the kind of self-motivated self-starters who don't need to be managed, leaving you free to take care of your most important responsibilities: profit, growth, and creating a company culture that will make you the envy of your competition.

Whether you are top management, middle management, or a business owner, I know you'll find my 9 Keys to Creating Self-Motivated High Achievers easy to understand and, more importantly, even easier to implement. When you follow this blueprint, I have no doubt you will start to see results almost immediately.

The 9 Keys I'll be covering are as follows:

1. People do things for their reasons, not yours.
2. Communicate great expectations!
3. Don't accept mediocrity: You set the standards and parameters.

4. Stop being a "jump out of the bushes" leader.
5. If you want them to listen to you, tell them they did something right.
6. Role models are important: The 10-80-10 rule.
7. Help your people build winning streaks.
8. Stop touching everything.
9. Help people understand the importance of their jobs.

As I did in my last book, *The Best Damn Sales Book Ever: 16 Rock-Solid Rules for Achieving Sales Success*, every once in a while I break away from the topic to give you either a Leadership Tip or a Rant, in order to expand on a point and give you more practical information that can be put to use immediately.

I also expound on my theory that a lot of the qualities necessary to be a good parent are the same qualities you need to be a good manager. I find the similarities amazing, except for one thing: You hear a lot more whining as a manager than you do as a parent.

This book is no magic formula. You are asked to do some work in order to get your people moving in the right direction. But don't worry, because everything I ask you to do, every idea I give you, is so easy to implement that you will have no excuse not to do it.

Chapter 1
Why You Need Self-Motivated People

M y all-time favorite New York Giants Football coach is Bill Parcells. Aside from the fact that he won two Super Bowls, his players always seemed to be willing to go through a brick wall for the guy. He had a reputation as a great motivator.

One day, at a press conference, when asked "What makes you such a great motivator?," Parcells said, "What makes me such a great motivator is, I only keep self-motivated players. If you're not self-motivated I cut you from the team."

Why You Need Self-Motivated People

Any successful manager, leader, coach, or teacher will tell you that you cannot motivate others on a long-term basis. Heck, I'm a motivational speaker. I can get in front of an audience, deliver a fire and brimstone, and in no time I'd have them swinging from the chandeliers. But 24 hours later they're gonna wake up and say, "Who was that guy?" Because that's external motivation and external motivation is a short-term fix.

The only kind of motivation that has a shot to last long-term is internal motivation. As a speaker, what I try to do is give my audience the tools and techniques that will allow them to be better able to motivate themselves. As a business owner, manager, or executive, if you really want to develop high achieving self-starters, you need to give them those same tools.

I've actually had managers and business owners tell me, "I get my people going every day. I kick 'em in the ass. That gets 'em going." Unfortunately, kicking people in the ass is not motivation: It's movement! And the problem with movement is: It eventually stops, and then your people are doing nothing, which means you constantly have to be around to keep kicking them. What important things are you not taking care of while you're running around kicking people in the ass?

Kicking people in the ass is called "external motivation," which is strictly a short-term fix. Internal motivation, the ability to motivate oneself, is a long-term solution.

As a manager or leader, there are three reasons you need self-motivated people.

1. You can't be around 24 hours a day making sure people are doing their jobs. First of all, you shouldn't be, because that means you're not doing your job. If you do not have self-motivated self-starters working for you, what is going on during the time you're not there? Probably not much. The question you need to ask yourself is: Do my people put forth as great an effort when I'm not there as they do when I'm around? If the answer to this is yes, you're doing your job as a leader.

5

Why You Need Self-Motivated People

2. It's critical to establishing extraordinary customer service. The delivery of extraordinary customer service requires a culture of excellence at every level, which is fostered by self-motivated workers with great attitudes. Remember, the people who report to you very often are the link between you and the customer. Their attitude toward the customer will be the customer's attitude toward your company.

3. Self-motivated people have the best attitudes.

Leadership Tip: Hire Attitude!

One of the questions I get most often from business owners and managers is: How do I find good people? What do I look for? I always say the same thing, "Hire attitude!"

Let's face it, you can probably teach someone everything they're going to need to know about the job and your company in what,

---

a matter of days? But it's a lot harder to teach someone a great attitude. And, if they don't have it coming into the job, what makes you think they're going to get it while they're on the job?

Sure, hiring people with great skills is nice. But without a great attitude those people won't use the skills, and if you don't use them you lose them. Conversely, someone with a great attitude and limited skills will not only run through a brick wall to acquire those skills, but they'll drive you crazy making sure you teach them the skills.

My best friend, Alan, whom you'll read about later, has a daughter named Sylvia. When Syl (that's what we call her) graduated from college, her goal was to be a corporate event planner and travel the world planning events and meetings. She had been in charge of putting on numerous events in college, was very good at it, and really loved it.

Of course, she knew she'd have to start at the bottom and work her way up. After a couple of low-level jobs in the insurance industry, she landed a job in Boston as an office manager with McKinsey & Company, the world's biggest global management consulting firm.

Now, in this case, office manager is one of those polite titles. Syl was really a combination assistant, office grunt, clerk, and slave. Among her many duties, she made sure there was always plenty of office supplies, ran errands, and kept the kitchen clean and well stocked. Not exactly a highly skilled job. Without the opportunity to impress people with her skills, Sylvia went them one better: She impressed them with her attitude!

No job was too small, menial, or insignificant for Sylvia. In fact, what brought her to the attention of the higher-ups was her willingness to do the one thing nobody else was willing to do: empty the dishwasher.

To make a long story short, she was promoted; Sylvia now reports to one of the top people in the company and guess what she's doing?—traveling the world putting on events and meetings for McKinsey. In fact, she just recently returned from trips to Poland, Paris, Germany, and Costa Rica. And she's done all this by the age of 28.

I wonder how many of you leaders out there have passed on hiring the Sylvias of the world because they didn't have the skills you were looking for.

Rant

To follow up on the Hire Attitude theme, I want to talk about a pet peeve of mine: people who look down on what others do for a living. They call jobs such as those at McDonald's, Wal-Mart—various nonskilled and even some skilled jobs—dead-end jobs. Fortunately, history has proven these white-collar snobs wrong, time and time again.

There is no such thing as a dead-end job, only people with dead-end attitudes. Put in the hands of a person with the right attitude, every

(Continued)

9

(Continued)

job, no matter how big or small, regardless of pay or stature, is an opportunity on a number of different levels, whether to:

- Show your stuff.
- Create a favorable impression.
- Get much-needed work experience.
- Learn responsibility.
- Get your foot in the door.
- Be in the right place at the right time, which can only be accomplished if you're in a lot of places, because you never know when someone will say, "I could use someone with your attitude."

I wonder how many successful executives, professionals, and entrepreneurs got their start in one of those dead-end hamburger flipping jobs at McDonald's. A job, any job, if nothing else, teaches you responsibility: Show up on time, show up every day, and work hard. What's so

bad about that? Everybody has to start some-
where. It's up to the person, not the job, whether
or not they stay there. That's why you hire
attitude!

Creating a staff of self-motivated people is going to save you a tremendous amount of time to
do the things you need to do in your job in order to achieve success for both you and your company. However, just like anything else that's going
to benefit you in the long run, there's a certain
amount of up-front work on your part that needs to
be done.

The best way to get started is to remember one
simple rule of thumb: Your staff, the people who
report to you, are your customers. Your attitude
toward them will be their attitude toward the customers and clients that buy from your company.
What are you doing to develop this internal client
base and instill in them the kind of attitude and
spirit that customers want to deal with? Whether
they work in customer service, sales, secretarial

Why You Need Self-Motivated People

support, accounting, installation, or the shipping department, each one of these people has the ability to make an impact on your company in either a positive or negative way. The choice is yours.

To start, let's go back to Sales 101. One of the first things salespeople are taught is: In order to develop high-quality long-term clients you need to talk to prospective clients, ask probing questions, uncover their needs, and then find a way to fill those needs on a consistent basis. It's the same way with your people—your internal clients. Probe for and uncover their needs. What are their goals and what would they like to achieve in their lives and careers? Once that's done, show them how they can use the job to achieve these goals.

The single biggest reason people are not self-motivated is: They themselves don't know what motivates them; they have no goals and no plan for either their life or career. I can't tell you how many times I've spoken at big corporate meetings where a CEO has gotten up in front of hundreds, if not thousands, of people and said something like, "If we put our noses to the grindstone and work real hard this year, this company will do great!" Then I look out into this sea of faces and they're all thinking to themselves, "Who cares! What's in it for me?"

Now here's the problem. If I were to go to each one of these people and ask them, "What do you want to be in it for you?," I guarantee 97 percent of them couldn't tell me. You can't motivate someone like that. There are far too many managers who say, "If I could only find the right hot button to push on this person." But you can't push a hot button on someone who has no buttons. One of your many jobs as a leader is to help your people find their buttons; this is part coaching hat and part motivator hat.

Setting goals and developing action plans is not a hard thing to do, but because most people have never done it, they assume it's difficult. So what happens? They do nothing. As their leader/coach/mentor and motivator, it is up to you to develop a relationship built on trust with your staff. Sit down, individually, with each of your people and listen, challenge, and support them through the process of developing and achieving both

13

Why You Need Self-Motivated People

their life and career goals. Also schedule quarterly review meetings to see what kind of progress they're making toward their goals.

People are motivated by the things they most want to accomplish—their goals, dreams, or aspirations. If they have no idea what those are or how they're going to achieve them, there is not one thing you can do to motivate them. How can they get excited about the *company's* success if they don't see how it contributes to *their* success?

Once you have helped them find their buttons and figure out what it is they want to achieve, you can then give them examples of how to use the job as a vehicle towards getting them what they want out of their lives and careers.

Now you have people who come to work knowing that "Every day that I come here and do my job to the best of my ability, I'm getting that much closer to what I want." Not only do they want to come to work every day, they can't wait to get there, because they know what it means to them; they're working for themselves. They no longer need you for every trivial thing and they're far more proactive than reactive. How much more productive do you think that will make you?

Once you've helped them find their buttons, there's still more work to do in order to install the self-starting generator in your people. Mostly, it's about how you communicate, and the kind of environment and culture you create in the workplace. So, as promised in the Introduction, the remaining chapters in this book will be dedicated to giving you "the 9 keys to creating self-motivated high achievers," allowing you to create a culture of excellence throughout your entire company.

Chapter 2

Key #1—People Do Things for Their Reasons, Not Yours

I have a good friend and fraternity brother, Dr. Alan Zaremba, who is a Professor of Communications at Northeastern University in Boston. Many years ago, to stay in shape, he started running. It almost became an obsession with him. He ran so much and so often that he started running marathons. When I asked why he was running so much and why marathons, he said, "So that I can eat like a pig." The moral of the story: Everybody is motivated by something different, and people do things for their reasons, not yours.

19

People Do Things for Their Reasons, Not Yours

Have you ever wondered why so many sales contests at your company don't work? Unless it's the big contests where trips to exotic locales are the prize, most people aren't motivated to participate.

First off, the same few salespeople win all the time. The rest of the people, knowing this, don't even try. True, there's no reason to diminish or punish top producers for being successful, but the whole point of a contest is to get everyone to increase sales. How about more contests based on improvement rather than overall production?

Second, many people don't try because the prizes stink. They're usually chosen based on what the manager or contest organizer likes, not on what the participants might actually want. This boils down to two things:

1. What I wrote about in Chapter 1: Treat each person who reports to you as a client. Find out what makes them tick, what they want and need. A free dinner at a nice restaurant to someone who eats out all the time is no

The Best Damn Management Book Ever

big deal. Same with a box of golf balls to someone who hates golf (like me!).

2. As a manager, executive, or business owner, assuming all the people who report to you are the same and are all motivated by the same things, is not only stupid, it's lazy and counterproductive.

Would you assume that all your clients are the same? Better yet, if you have kids, especially if you have more than one, I'll bet there's no way you can tell me your kids are exactly the same.

I know my kids, Michael, 24, and Emily, 20, are as different as night and day. Michael is part leader, part nonconformist. He'll do something just because nobody else is doing it. I'm convinced that if under-age drinking and illegal drugs were something high school kids *never* did, Michael would have been stumbling home drunk and high every day. Luckily the opposite was true.

Emily, on the other hand, is a follower, and while she's gotten much better since starting college, she's still much more comfortable as part of a

People Do Things for Their Reasons, Not Yours

group. She's extremely social (all right, she likes to party), has had boyfriends (notice the plural) since ninth grade, is a member of a sorority, and is far more likely to let someone else lead.

Michael, while a friendly and well-liked person who maintains a small circle of friends, is a bit anti-social. He has no problem doing things on his own. When he was in college, no way he was joining a frat. He lives by himself in an apartment in New York. He likes to go to concerts, restaurants, and movies by himself.

Michael is so cheap he can make a dollar bill yell Uncle. He not only supports himself in New York City on an entry-level salary, but he's saving money. Emily has a black belt in shopping.

Michael likes baseball, music, and eating (a lot). Emily likes shopping, Broadway musicals, hanging out with her sorority sisters, and going to frat parties.

Does this make one kid better than the other? No way. They're both great kids. It just means they're different and they're motivated by different things.

When Michael graduated high school, his gift from his parents was a trip to San Francisco to see the Giants play (three games; we won two), and stuff his face in some great restaurants.

When Emily graduated from high school, we took her to London, where she had a great time spending a week visiting with her brother (who was there on a study abroad program), hitting every store on Oxford Street, and seeing *Jersey Boys*.

Each of these trips was tailored to what the person being rewarded would like. I'm sure you tailor your sales presentations to what your clients and prospects want and need. Why not tailor rewards and contests to what your internal customers want, like, and need?

If all your incentives and rewards are the same for everyone, how do you get anyone excited about it? Guaranteed there's a huge percentage of your staff who couldn't care less about contests you might think are fantastic.

If you're not willing to invest some time knowing what makes each one of your people tick, the same way you spend time trying to understand the specific needs of each client, why should your people care one bit about the needs of the company or the clients?

Because I've been on both sides of the fence as an employee, a manager, and, for the last 25 years, a business owner, I'm pretty attuned to all the excuses and negative comments I'm going to hear about my ideas.

Leadership Rant

I can't tell you how many small business owners have said to me, "Why should I bother to train and develop my people; they're only gonna leave me for a better job?" Great! So instead of having self-motivated high achievers whom the customers would love, you'd rather have mediocre morons working for you because they'll never leave. How could they leave? Who in their right mind would want them? By the way, how are your customers enjoying dealing with mediocrities?

Here's a question for you: What's so bad about being known as a company where workers can get the kind of training and development that will enable them to go on to bigger and better things?

I don't get it: Every company I speak to, especially if it's a small business, is constantly moaning about the lack of good people with tons of ambition, strong work ethic, and great attitudes. Let's face it; workers like Sylvia are the exception, not the norm.

If you were one of those companies where young people go on to bigger and better things, don't you think it would be a lot easier for you to find and recruit good people? Heck, I imagine they'd be beating down your door.

Another common excuse I hear, not only from business owners but also managers and executives is: "I don't have to find out what motivates them. I know what motivates them: *money*! They just want more money."

People Do Things for Their Reasons, Not Yours

Well, yeah, sure, everyone wants more money. Nobody is ever going to tell you they want less money. But if you think money is going to motivate people into doing a better job, you're crazy.

Think about this: Did you ever work at a job you really hated? I'm sure every person reading this would say yes to that question, including me. Now, even though you hated the job, did you ever receive a raise on that job? I know I did, and I'm sure many of you did too. However, when you came to work the next day, the day after receiving the raise, did you now love the job or did you still hate it? I'm betting you still hated the job.

You see, money is not something that makes us love our jobs; it's just something that might stop us, temporarily, from hating our jobs. Nobody ever wakes up in the morning and says, "I can't wait to get to work today, because they pay me well." But, you might hear people say this, "I hate this job! I'd love to get out of here, but they pay me well so I might as well stay." Wow, talk about commitment! Wouldn't you love to have someone like that

26

working for you? They act as if they're doing you a favor by taking your money.

Companies give workers many things that they feel should motivate the employees to greater performance, yet they only accomplish one thing: They stop them from hating the job.

Just as with money, nobody ever wakes up in the morning and says, "I can't wait to get to work today because we have great health benefits." Or, "I can't wait to get to work today because I love our company's new policy on vacation days."

You know what really motivates people in the workplace to love their jobs?: achievement, recognition, the work itself. That's what makes people wake up in the morning wanting to come to work.

My good friend and ex-college roommate, Bobby, was an elementary school teacher in New Jersey for about 35 years. He retired in 2010, not because he wanted to but because budget cuts might have threatened his pension if he didn't retire. When I asked him why he waited so long to retire, he said, "I love teaching." It had nothing to

27

do with the money. He just liked doing it. Coincidentally, because he loved it so much, he was a fantastic teacher. Funny how that works, isn't it?

My son Michael graduated from college in May 2010. A month later he fulfilled a life-long ambition by landing a job in the music business at Decca Records in New York City. However, after the first few months, he seemed pretty disillusioned and his attitude didn't seem very good, at least not to me.

He was complaining about the bad state of the industry—which is true. Because of so many people pirating music online, sales in the industry have been suffering for years. There was a round of lay-offs at Decca, which he survived, but he wasn't busy enough and he seemed convinced there was no future for a young person in the music business.

Six months later his tune and attitude did a complete 180-degree turn. What did it, you ask? While he wasn't crazy about the job, Michael continued to work hard and do good work and he was recognized for it, not with more money but with a lot of added responsibility. He was being kept busy and he loved it! Plus, all of a sudden he believed there just might be some opportunity in this business. Recognition and responsibility can be very powerful motivators.

Money is not a motivator. Money is a vehicle. It is a vehicle that allows us to live the type of lifestyle we choose to live. So what do we really need to know? Of course, what type of lifestyle do we want to live? In fact, if your people can answer the question, "How do I want my life to look?" that will tell you how much money they need to make. Once you know that amount, you can help them formulate a plan to get it. Only if we know what we're going to do with the money is there any motivation to get it.

Once a person has a clear idea of how their job, and the money they earn can be a vehicle towards helping them achieve the life they want, their attitude and performance on the job will improve because now they're working for themselves and their ultimate goal.

Chapter 3

Key #2—Communicate Great Expectations!

The best teacher I've ever seen is a woman named Diane Lorber. Diane was Michael's teacher in both the third and fourth grades (September 1995 to June 1997) at PS 11 in Manhattan. She taught what was then called the gifted track. Each student in her class had to qualify by reaching a certain level on a standardized test. I must admit, though, there were quite a few kids in the class who didn't seem very gifted.

As impressive as that sounds, PS 11 was your typical overcrowded inner-city public school. I

Communicate Great Expectations!

won't say underfunded, because there's plenty of money in the system; it just doesn't always get to the classroom.

Ms. Lorber had 27 students in her class. No teaching assistant. One computer that was horrendously outdated. A dot-matrix printer that didn't work, no textbooks (she photocopied homework sheets for all 27 kids every day), and hardly any paper. She paid for supplies and books out of her own pocket. The only reason she had a set of encyclopedias in the classroom was that I, after keynoting the annual sales meeting for World Book, convinced them to donate a set of encyclopedias to Ms. Lorber's class.

What made her so great was her ability to communicate expectations and inspire the kids to believe they could reach those expectations. She demanded more out of these kids than they'd ever done before. But she also let them know, every day, that she had 100 percent confidence in their ability to do it.

Even though this was a "gifted" class, Ms. Lorber consistently taught above curriculum. She challenged them every day. She let it be known that not only did she expect everyone in the class to do great work, she also had supreme confidence in their ability to do it. Some of the kids had trouble keeping up at the beginning, but by the end of the year, every one of them was working far beyond not only their own expectations but even those of their parents!

During the school year there was an open house at PS 11, giving the parents a chance to have Ms. Lorber address us and tell us what was going on. I was amazed at how many parents loudly complained about the workload and how hard she was on their kids. I felt so bad for her that I finally got up and said, "Hey, this is supposed to be a gifted class. If your kid can't keep up, maybe he or she is not very gifted. Let the woman do her job."

To this day, I'm still amazed that there were parents whose expectations for their own children weren't nearly as high as Ms. Lorber's. When you expect the best from people and not only communicate that fact, but let them know you

Communicate Great Expectations!

have confidence they can do it, you'll be amazed at how often you get the best. The opposite is also true.

Have you ever witnessed a parent who tells a child, "You'll never amount to anything. Everything you touch turns to crap"? Then, some years later they get a call telling them their kid's been arrested and they're amazed. What are you amazed about? You predicted it! You should be proud. You were right!

I've known business owners who complain they can't afford to go on vacation because they're afraid of what might happen while they're away. They don't trust their own people, which is ironic since they're the one who hired these people. I could never understand how you can hire someone to do a job but, at the same time, not trust them to do it. It's obvious the problem is not with the workers.

Years ago, I had a boss whose name was Sal. Sal taught me everything about what *not* to do in order to be a great leader and manager. He held sales meetings Friday afternoon at 5:30 P.M.

His purpose was to ruin our weekends. Every meeting started the same way. We would sit in his office, silently, while he sat behind his desk staring at us for about 30 seconds. Finally, he'd look up and say, "I just want youse guys [Brooklyn native] to know, youse all suck!"

Aside from being General Sales Manager overseeing four divisions (I was Sales Manager of one of those divisions), Sal also was the top producing salesperson, though there should have been an asterisk next to that designation. He never allowed his salespeople to do for their customers many of the things he routinely did for his, such as returning merchandise that didn't sell and helping them pay for markdowns that might incur. In other words, Sal perpetrated one of the greatest crimes a manager can commit against his or her people: He made himself look good at others' expense.

In fact, I'll go you one even better. Sal once said to me, "Never tell anyone they're doing a good job." I thought this was the opening straight line to a joke, so I played along and said, "Why?" He said,

Communicate Great Expectations!

in all seriousness, "Because they're liable to ask you for a raise."

While his expectations were high, he never gave anyone the feeling that he had the slightest bit of confidence in their ability to reach those expectations. And, when we didn't, he took great joy in his ability to predict our failures.

What a motivator! You just wanted to run through a brick wall for this guy. He was so clueless that one day he had the nerve to ask me, "Why is our turnover so high?" What did he expect? People will *always* rise or fall to your level of communicated expectation.

There are far too many Sals out there, and that's a good reason why so many companies are not successful. You'll be happy to know there is justice in the world and, thanks to Sal's brilliant leadership, the company eventually went belly up.

But, luckily, there are a lot of great managers and leaders out there, which brings me to my best friend, Alan Weinstock. For the past three years Alan has been the President and CEO of PSCH, a large nonprofit health care agency in Queens, New York.

Before going to PSCH, Alan spent over 30 years working for the State of New York and the State Office of Mental Health. He had numerous positions, including Deputy Commissioner. He spent many years as Executive Director of numerous state mental institutions, with the bulk of those years being spent as Executive Director of Pilgrim State Mental Institution on Long Island, the largest mental hospital in the United States. It was here I first noticed his talents as a great manager and leader.

Alan took me on a tour of Pilgrim State one Sunday to show me some of the improvements and new programs he had put in. You can spruce it up as much as you want, but to a neophyte like me, touring a mental institution is dreary, depressing, and downright scary.

We walked into an area where there must have been 100 inmates/patients milling around or working on projects. I wanted to dive for cover, hoping one of them wouldn't go berserk.

I was looking for Alan when I noticed him walking through the crowd of people, smiling, laughing, shaking hands, listening to problems and suggestions, and telling stories as if he were running for Senate. To him, these weren't just inmates or patients; they were customers.

He was the same way with his staff, from the lowest orderly to his deputy directors. Everyone received his time and attention, and no request, idea, or suggestion was treated as if it were unimportant.

At the time I wondered, "Why is he working for the state when he could be doing and accomplishing so much more and not have to answer to a bunch of bureaucrats."

Alan left the state's employ five years ago to become Executive Vice President of PSCH. Unfortunately, the President and CEO at the time was someone who made Sal look like Rebecca of Sunnybrook Farm. This was the boss from hell, but before he could drag the whole place down, the Board got rid of him and put Alan in his place.

Leadership Alert—Egoless Management

What really makes Alan unique as a leader, is: He has perfected what I call Egoless Management. He doesn't care about getting credit or receiving accolades. He's far more concerned with performance and excellent results. He couldn't care less if his people outshine him, because he takes pride in the fact that he's the one who hired them. He doesn't have to demand respect, because he earns it.

He brings in the best people he knows. I've seen him turn down his own raises so he could bring in top people. He lets everyone know what's expected of them, but also lets them know he has confidence that they'll more than fulfill those expectations. He doesn't micromanage and he *always, always* gives his staff the credit.

(Continued)

Communicate Great Expectations!

(*Continued*)

Bottom line: Since Alan took over as President and CEO three years ago, the company has grown from $58 to $130 million. In a bad economy, no less!

If you ever hope to develop self-motivated high achievers, it's not enough for them to have confidence in themselves. You have to communicate the fact that you have 100 percent confidence in them too.

Of course, I'll bet there are people who work for you who'd prefer to operate with low expectations. It's not that they can't rise to the occasion, it's just that fear of failure stops them and, even worse, you've bought into their mediocre performance and have accepted it.

The same thing happened to my wife, Linda, and me with our daughter, Emily, until one fateful night. Here's the background.

Emily has just finished her sophomore year at High Point University in High Point, North Carolina, and is doing great. Her grades are better than they've ever been (all As and Bs). She is an active member of a sorority; has a job on campus; is active in campus activities; and is really taking advantage of the entire college experience. In addition, she's a pleasure to be around and is just a really great kid, who I have high hopes for. However, that wasn't always the case.

From eighth grade through high school Emily was a swift pain in the butt. She was your typical surly, moody teenager. As a student she was, at best, disinterested or, at worst, the part of the class that makes the top half possible. Have you ever gone to a parent/teacher conference and asked your kid just before you walk in, "How's it going in this class?" The kid says "Fine," and then the first thing the teacher hits you with is, "Emily is missing 11 assignments!" Don't you love those conversations?

Normal conversations (both mine and Linda's) with Emily would go like this: "How's school, Em?" "Fine." "Anything happen today?" "No." "Have any homework?" "A little." There were the screaming

Communicate Great Expectations!

matches, too. "I hate you." "You hate me." "None of my friends ever have to do that." Or, of course, "My friends get to do (or have) _____, why can't I?" That one bugged me so much I finally said, "Hey, Em, how come you never say, "My friends get all A's, how come I don't?"

There was the usual sneaking out of the house stuff. The friends we never got to meet and the ones we did know but weren't crazy about, and of course, the boys (it didn't help that Em is a very pretty girl). To sum it up, Em was a "Valley Girl" who was going to major in "Shopping Mall."

We threatened her; punished her; grounded her; took away privilege upon privilege; bailed her out (not jail, but school); and let her sink. Finally, we just threw up our hands and said, "Well, at least she didn't fail. A C is not bad." She had worn us down. We had low expectations and Emily was happy to fulfill them. She loved playing the dumb, clueless blond. But then, late in her senior year of high school, it all changed.

The Turning Point

For 11 years Emily had been a member and captain of the Bouncing Bulldogs Rope Skipping Team. Every year the team has an end of year banquet, where the graduating seniors give a speech. In Em's senior year she was one of five girls graduating; three of them were top students going on to big time schools. Linda and I were worried that Em was going to fall on her face.

I told her I would not write the speech for her but I'd help her with the editing and coach her. Two days before the banquet I asked how the speech was coming. She screamed, "I don't know what to write." Finally, I told her just write what you feel. Talk about your experiences and all the friends you've made.

The next day Emily hands me a copy of the speech to edit. I was blown away. I said to Linda, "You're not going to believe this, it's great! There's nothing to edit." I told Em I loved it, gave her two to three minutes of coaching, and that was it.

Communicate Great Expectations!

The night of the banquet she blew the place away. It was amazing. She was funny, poignant, and poised. Eye contact: perfect. Ability to deliver a punch line: phenomenal. There were people asking me if I wrote it (nope). Did I coach her for weeks (nope, three minutes). It was all Emily.

The next day I sat her down and said, "Em, you blew your cover. The jig is up. After that performance you will never again convince us that you can't do *anything* you put your mind to. The dumb blonde routine is not going to work on your mother and me, because last night, you blew it.

"So here's the deal," I said. "The bar has been raised and you're the one who raised it. From now on a C is not acceptable. Your mother and I will only accept A and B work because we've seen the kind of A+ work you're capable of. You blew away every one of those girls who were supposed to be smarter and more articulate than you."

As I stated earlier, Emily knocked it out of the park her freshman year, so I sat her down and we decided to raise the bar ever higher in this, her sophomore year, and she's living up to all the expectations and more, which is no surprise to me.

Far too many people in this world suffer from the disease of low expectations. Whether you're a parent, manager, business owner, teacher, or anyone else in a leadership position, expect the best from people. Communicate that fact to them and let them know that you know they are more than capable of doing and being the best, and you'll be amazed at how often you get the best. That too is a self-fulfilling prophecy.

Communicate Great Expectations!

Chapter 4

Key #3—Don't Accept Mediocrity: You Set the Standards and Parameters

My son Michael started his college career in 2005 at Western Carolina University. After one year he decided he hated it and wanted to transfer. He applied to and was accepted at the University of North Carolina at Greensboro. However, at the summer orientation program, it was obvious that transfer students were being treated like garbage. For example, during this "Orientation" session they had an Information Fair set up with booths representing different departments and activities on campus such as housing, various academic departments, extracurricular activities, etc. The only problem was, in at least half of the booths there was nobody manning them, so if you had any questions or inquiries you were out of luck.

In one of the information sessions Michael and I attended, the speaker failed to show up and to top it all off we found out, at the last second, that Michael would not have a dorm room. When we went to the housing department, the head of housing, who at first refused to talk to us, said, "Go find an apartment off campus," and turned around and walked away.

I often wonder: why would anyone give money to an organization that treats you like a second class citizen before they've even gotten their hands on your money? Can you imagine what would happen once they had your money? Michael decided he had no desire to go there (I didn't blame him), and said to me, "Dad, would you mind if I dropped out and took a year off?"

Since I learned a long time ago, as both a parent and a business owner, that you don't put people into situations they're not ready for and where they're doomed to fail, I said, "No problem, but there are two conditions. One, you need to get a full-time job. Two, you pay me rent." Michael agreed to the terms ($200 a month rent) and got a job delivering pizzas for a local pizza parlor.

He spent a year on the job, made a lot of money, saved a lot of money, invested it wisely, and learned many invaluable lessons, such as handling responsibility, showing up every day and showing up on time, how to deal with both nice and irate customers, how to manage his money, and how to deal with people from backgrounds far different from his. And, by the way, he paid his rent on time every month.

After a year of reality, he decided to go back to college and enrolled at Elon University, where he graduated three years later. As I mentioned earlier, he's now a marketing coordinator at Decca Records and living on his own in New York City.

It's amazing, as a parent, how much I learn about being a better business owner/leader and, as a business owner/leader, how much I learn about being a better parent. Just as everyone is motivated by something different, not everyone's pace, adaptability curve, or learning curve is the same.

Just because Michael did not take the traditional route didn't mean he wasn't going to get to where he eventually needed and wanted to be. You must understand that the same thing will happen with many of the people who report to you. Just because it seems to take them a little longer, or they're not doing it the way you would, don't give up on them. Understand them and realize they'll achieve the results you want; they'll just take a different path to get there. Support them along that path and you'll have yourself a self-motivated high achiever.

One of the keys as a business leader, just as it was with me as a parent, is your responsibility to set the standards and parameters. And when I say "set the standards," I mean high standards. People need to know what level of excellence is expected of them.

However, just because you're setting high standards of performance, quality, and even behavior, doesn't mean you need to be a rigid dictator whose mind is closed to any ideas but his own. Remember, innovation is not a top-down phenomenon. Real innovation always comes from the bottom up. It comes from the people closest to the action.

Great managers or leaders encourage innovation and new ideas by giving their people freedom within the standards and parameters that are set. Think of a boxing ring, and imagine that the ropes on all four sides of the ring are the standards and parameters you want your people to work within. However, once inside that ring you want to encourage them to move in any direction they choose. In the best-run companies a certain amount of individuality is not only tolerated, but encouraged. You never want to squash creativity. Unfortunately, that happens all too often in today's business world.

Leadership Tip—Allow Your People to Make Decisions

As a customer, I don't think there's anything more frustrating than a customer service rep or

(Continued)

(*Continued*)

salesperson with no decision-making capability. The last thing a customer with a problem wants to hear is that they're going to have to wait for someone else (who can actually make a decision) to get back to them. What makes it even more frustrating is:

- Most customers believe no one will ever call them back. Past experience tells us that; and they believe they will have to waste even more time following up on this. Or,
- Instead of having to wait for a call that may never come, when the customer asks for a name of someone to call, they're often told: "Sorry, we can't give out that information."

I don't know about you, but I have pretty much cut out dealing with companies whose executives tell us, by their actions, that they have no desire to get their hands dirty and actually talk to a customer. I'm convinced that many companies set up elaborate customer service departments in order to make these poor reps a buffer between corporate headquarters and the customers.

One of the major reasons the people who are closest to the customers don't get to make decisions is: Their managers or employers are afraid they'll make too many mistakes and give customers more than they're entitled to.

My answer is: So what? Sure they're going to make mistakes; doesn't everybody? (And, by the way, it's really hard to give a customer, especially a good one, too much.) How else do we learn but by doing, and making mistakes? It's up to the manager, leader, or owner of the company to help these people correct their mistakes and learn from the experience.

Pushing decision-making responsibility as far down as possible insures quicker decisions;

(Continued)

Don't Accept Mediocrity

(*Continued*)

faster resolutions to customer problems and complaints; more motivated workers, since added responsibility has been found to be one of the primary causes of people loving their jobs; and naturally happy customers who will most certainly come back and do even more business with you in the future.

Which do you think is harder to find: companies who encourage their people to make decisions and resolve customer problems, or companies who don't? Obviously, from experience, we know the answer is that those who do are much harder to find. If that's the case, why be one of the companies who don't, because by being a company who does, you'll be in the minority; you'll stand out and easily differentiate yourself from the competition. This gives you a tremendous opportunity to increase your business and especially your market share. And in these crazy times, market share is king!

As you can well imagine, my old boss, Sal, was great at squashing innovation. He was one of those awful managers who believed any idea that didn't come from him was no good. Anytime one of us would actually bother to come to him with a good idea he would always say the same thing: "That's a good idea, but we're going to do it our way." If you hear that enough times, eventually you know what happens: People stop coming up with good ideas, which, in time, will turn your company into one stagnant mess.

The company that I would crown the King of Innovation has to be 3M. Not just because of the constant stream of new and innovative products they always seem to come up with, but because they encourage innovation more than most other companies and they have a plan for innovation that clearly defines the standards and parameters of bringing new ideas to market (See *Innovation White Paper*, by Paul Davis, January 2008; www.hope.edu/admin/frost/Assets/InnovationWhitePaper.pdf).

3M encourages its people to run with their new product ideas and gives them the support to do it. However, unless the new product produces a certain amount of revenue or profitability within a certain amount of time, it's back to square one. Of course, if the product does achieve the clearly defined standards and parameters laid out, it gets split into its own division or company.

Accepting mediocrity will create a lazy culture throughout your entire company. Sure, there are always going to be people who will be high achievers, but the vast majority are members of the "Give them an inch and they'll take a foot" club. Once they know they can slide by, that's what they're going to do (Don't your kids do the same thing if you let them?). You know as well as I do that most people would rather put forth minimum effort and do okay than have to put forth maximum effort in order to be successful.

It all comes back to the fact that most people don't know what it takes to be successful, because they can't define what they want to achieve and therefore are going through life without a road map. I can't emphasize enough how much you need to help them develop that road map.

A consistent culture of high standards and well-defined parameters is the mark of any great company or organization. What do you think made McDonald's the powerhouse it is today and has been for many years?

There are a lot of factors that made McDonald's the number one company in their industry. First of all, they put the "fast" in fast food. They were one of the first, if not the very first, to understand that speed, convenience, and ease were more important to their customers than food. They were far ahead of the competition in understanding what customers wanted. It took 18 years for the competition to copy McDonalds' highly successful Happy Meal.

But to me, what really helped McDonald's stand out was their consistency. It didn't matter where you were in the world; it didn't matter whether you had ever been to that location—before you even walked in the door you knew what it would smell like, look like, taste like, and cost, and you knew the store would be clean and the service courteous.

Can your clients and customers expect the same consistency of performance out of every department, branch, or individual in your company? When clients call and ask three different people the same question, do they get three different answers, or is everyone on the same page?

If I walked into any one of your offices, stores, or locations, would I be greeted, treated, and responded to in the same fast, courteous way by people who give me the impression they really want to be there?

Is there a culture of excellence along with a standard operating procedure for each job and/or function in your company, right down to how you answer the phones?

Clients hate surprises and most people have a huge fear of the unknown. If your service and people are totally inconsistent depending on the location, don't be surprised when clients avoid those locations where "You never know what to expect."

Many of you reading this might be saying, "I'm doing all this stuff." Or, "Our location (branch, store) is doing everything we're supposed to do and more. It's not my fault if the other people or locations aren't doing it."

You're right; it's not your fault. But poor service, performance, or attitude by others in your company, even though they might be located hundreds of miles from you, still impacts you in a negative way. It diminishes the reputation of your company in a client's mind and perpetuates a perception of poor attitude, performance, and service to people who have yet to deal with you, but now may never do so.

Since the performance of each individual within an organization impacts the performance of everyone else, if you are one of the people who is doing it right, it now becomes your responsibility to make sure everyone else does it right too.

Don't Accept Mediocrity

Chapter 5

Key #4—Stop Being a "Jump Out of the Bushes" Leader!

S al loved to catch us doing something wrong. You could do 100 things right and never hear about it, but do just one thing wrong and he'd pounce like a starving mountain lion, screaming his head off and saying, "I knew you'd screw up." It wasn't exactly a relaxed atmosphere.

Here's how clueless he was. Our hours were 8:30 A.M. to 5:30 P.M. One day he calls me into his office and tells me he's extending the hours to 5:45. Why, you ask? He was mad that people were

Stop Being a "Jump Out of the Bushes" Leader!

leaving at exactly 5:30 and not hanging around or staying late voluntarily. So to make sure they did that, he extended the workday by 15 minutes. Was this guy insane or what?

He never understood, no matter how much I told him, that people will never voluntarily hang around a place where they don't want to be.

You could set your watch by this place. At exactly 8:30 every morning people filed through the door. Not a minute early and not a minute late. Every night at exactly 5:45 everyone left.

Before I had the motivation beaten out of me, I used to stay late once or twice a week to call my West Coast clients. Since my clients were all large retailers, I very often came in on Saturday morning to call them. Knowing no one else would be calling, they'd have plenty of time to talk, were probably catching up on paperwork, and would be thrilled to talk to me.

One day, I came in 15 minutes late and Sal raked me over the coals. I said, "Hey, what is this crap? I come in early, I leave late, and work on Saturdays."

He said, "You're supposed to do that. That's what we pay you for."

At that point I decided, like everyone else who worked there, that since narrow-minded policy and process were far more important than results, I would do the minimum. I'd follow the rules. I'd arrive on time, leave on time, and do my job—nothing more, and nothing less.

The problem with that is: Doing what you're supposed to do when you're supposed to do it will get you an A in school, but in the real world it's only worth a C.

Sal had created a culture of fear, and fear is a demotivator. Fear stops people from doing more than they're capable of doing. Fear of failure is the biggest obstacle to success. At Sal's company, (Amy Deb Fashions), fear of getting yelled at, criticized, or treated like an idiot created an entire company of people whose only goal was not to do anything wrong and be noticed.

The problem is that it's almost impossible to do something right if you never do anything wrong. In

Stop Being a "Jump Out of the Bushes" Leader!

order for a company to be great, people have to be willing to take risks and go above and beyond. If your fear of making a mistake and being singled out is greater than the possible thrill of success, you end up doing nothing. Imagine if an entire company of people just stops and does the minimum. I've been there and it's not a pretty sight.

You have to let go and allow your people to make mistakes. The first step is to create a culture and environment where mistakes and failure are not a death penalty.

The ability to make mistakes is how people learn and gain valuable experience. We learn far more from our mistakes than we do from doing nothing. However, if you're going to allow and encourage your people to move beyond their self-imposed limitations and make mistakes, the one thing you have to be sure of is that they don't make the same mistakes over and over again. That is not a learning experience.

Another one of your responsibilities as a manager is to point out the mistakes people make and show them how to correct those mistakes. Of course, that brings up another dilemma: constructive criticism.

I honestly believe there is no such thing as constructive criticism. It's pretty much the same as saying to someone, "Don't take this personally but. . . ." You know that, no matter what you say next, they're going to take it personally. Why? Because everything in life is personal.

Let's face it: We're far more motivated by our personal goals than career and business goals. While those goals are important, they're more a means to an end. Most times, they're the vehicle that allows us to live the life we choose to live. Every criticism is rejection, and as someone who has been in sales for almost 40 years, I know that rejection is personal.

Okay, I know what you're thinking. Here's this crazy person telling you, on one hand, that you have to allow your people to make mistakes as long as you take time to point them out and show them how to fix those mistakes. Yet, on the other hand, he's saying there's no such thing as constructive criticism, and it's going to be extremely hard

Stop Being a "Jump Out of the Bushes" Leader!

to not only get people to correct their mistakes, but to just listen to your criticism. So, what do you do?

Well, there's really only one thing you can do, and that takes us to Chapter 6 and Key #5.

Chapter 6

Key #5—If You Want Them to Listen to You, Tell Them They Did Something Right

The title of this chapter says it all. If you want the right to point out the mistakes people make and get them to listen to you and fix those mistakes, you'd better be ready to recognize them when they do something right.

As I stated earlier, recognition is one of the greatest motivators in the workplace. Do you know anyone who doesn't like to be recognized when they've done something right or achieved something special?

Tell Them They Did Something Right

Let's face it: Incentives work. By recognizing someone for a job well done, you're giving them one hell of a great reason to listen to you when you point out and correct their mistakes. If one of your people makes a mistake, but knows, from past experience, that he or she will be recognized for correcting that mistake, they're far more likely to listen to what you have to say and act on the advice.

From the time I was a kid in high school until I was in my early thirties, I was convinced that I was a lousy writer. Why? Because that's all I was ever told, by teachers, friends, parents, and people I worked for.

I'll admit the stuff I wrote was crap, but it sure would have been nice if, instead of just criticizing, someone had shown me how to do it better. I reached the point where I flat-out hated to write. When I decided to change careers, I went to a career counseling office and hired them to write a resume for me.

That attitude changed when I made the career change in 1983. I went to work as Sales Manager for a small consulting company in New York City. The owner of the company forced me to write a thank-you letter every time I came back from a sales appointment.

He taught me about the correct structure of letters, how to phrase them, and what to say to get the reaction I wanted. He also gave me a tremendous amount of positive feedback every time I wrote another letter. The more letter writing I did, the better I got at it. Funny how that works, isn't it?

Before long I started writing proposals, speeches, and even short articles. Finally I started to think I was pretty good at this.

Now here we are, 28 years later, and you're currently reading my second book, published by John Wiley & Sons, a high-powered publishing house. I've written thousands of articles, blog posts, podcast scripts, radio shows, and speeches. I've been published in magazines and trade journals all over the world and I get paid to write articles. All this happened because someone took the time to give me constructive criticism balanced by praise, recognition, and positive reinforcement.

Tell Them They Did Something Right

I wonder how many people on your staff have a talent that they themselves are not aware of because nobody—manager, coach, teacher, parent—has bothered to help them recognize and develop it. And better yet, what if that talent is something that can positively affect the performance of your company?

The past two years in a row, Alan has brought me in as the featured speaker at his company's annual retreat. Two years ago I spoke to his top management team. Last year I addressed the entire management team.

What has impressed me most about the people at PSCH is their total commitment to thinking outside the box. Remember, while innovation comes from the bottom up, company culture comes from the top down. Alan has created a culture that encourages outside the box thinking, something that is extremely unusual in the nonprofit healthcare agency business.

With the federal government taking over health care, combined with inevitable cuts in government funded programs like Medicaid and Medicare, non-profit health care agencies across the country will see certain revenue streams shrink. What have most of these agencies done? The same thing they've always done, while still expecting the same result: which as we know, is a true definition of insanity.

PSCH, on the other hand, encourages their people to come up with ideas for new businesses, new revenue streams, and ways to deliver treatment more cost effectively and efficiently while maintaining high quality care. In three years, Alan has changed the culture from one of fear to one of growth, excitement, and doing things right—the PSCH way. Coincidentally, PSCH continues to grow while gobbling up other agencies along the way.

Tell Them They Did Something Right

Chapter 7

Key #6—Role Models Are Important:
The 10/80/10 Rule

When asked the key to being a successful manager, the late Billy Martin, former manager of the New York Yankees baseball team, replied: "Of the 25 players on your roster, one-third love you, one-third hate you, and the other third are on the fence. The key to being a successful manager is to keep the one-third on the fence away from the one-third who hate you."

The keys to being a successful manager in the business world are not much different. Like sports teams, most staffs break down into three groups:

Role Models Are Important: The 10/80/10 Rule

10 percent of your people are fantastic, they're your top producers; 10 percent are awful, they should be kicked down the stairs and out the door; and the other 80 percent are totally average. The difference between the successful and unsuccessful manager is how he or she deals with all three groups.

Again, let's remember—the single, biggest commodity that managers have the least of is *time*! You, as a manager, are responsible for recruiting, training, motivating, planning, budgeting, and God knows what else. If you are a sales manager, you may also be responsible for personal production.

The last thing you need is to waste time with people who either don't need you or aren't getting any better no matter how much time you spend with them. So let's examine these three disparate groups and see where your time is best spent.

The Top 10 Percent

The best thing you, as a manager, can do for the top 10 percent is: *Leave them alone!* They don't need you to push them. They're self-motivated;

that's what makes them top producers. The best way to manage these people is to walk up to them once a week and say, "You're doing a great job! Anything I can do for you? No? Great! See you next week."

Too many managers need to touch and control everything. They worry that if they're not constantly involved with a salesperson or staff member, they won't get credit for that person's success. Don't worry about who gets credit. When that person succeeds, the credit you deserve will show up in your compensation. Many managers have ruined top producers because they couldn't bring themselves to leave them alone and let them do the job they were hired to do.

This doesn't mean you shouldn't keep track of your top people. You must be on the lookout for signs of falling production or sliding work quality. No matter how much top producers like being left alone, when they stop being a top producer, they give up that privilege. I have no problem treating someone like a superstar as long as he or she continues performing like a superstar.

Leadership Alert—You Want to Be Treated Like a Superstar, Produce Like One

Lawrence Taylor was the greatest football player I've ever seen. He played for the New York Giants from 1981 through 1993. Before he came to the team they were garbage. After he retired, they were garbage again, and in between they won two Super Bowls and he forever changed the way the game is played.

Some of the other players on the team would complain to Coach Parcells or George Young, the VP and general manager, about the special treatment LT would receive. They would very simply reply, "You play like LT, you'll get the same special treatment." Case closed.

Sports teams and businesses are not democracies; they're meritocracies, where your progress is based on talent, ability, and most of all, results!

The Bottom of the Barrel

Now for the second group: the 10 percent who should be kicked down the stairs and out the door. Get rid of them! They're killing your team and you don't have time to perform miracles. Sure, every executive reading this article can tell me a story of the one they saved. But how about the 99.9 percent who weren't saved, and how many potentially good ones did you lose because you were devoting inordinate amounts of time to people who weren't going to improve?

As noted earlier, managers have many responsibilities. Your time is not infinite. There's no time to be a savior. The odds of turning around a nonproducer are way too slim. Besides, you can replace that level of production with a stick.

The Middle of the Pack

It's the middle group, the 80 percent who are average, who need your help and attention. These are people who can go either way. Imagine how much your sales or efficiency would increase if all you did was get 10 percent of that middle 80 percent to move toward the top group. Remember, all the time you waste trying to be a savior to a bottom 10 percenter is time you could have used helping someone in this middle group who has a better shot at improving.

Leadership Tip: Use Role Models and Mentors

One thing you might consider to get the middle 80 percent moving upward is role models; especially those within your own company.

As much as I admire great figures in history like Winston Churchill, Martin Luther King, Mother Teresa, and Gandhi, it's hard to sell them to your people as role models, since none of your people believe they're ever going to become the next Churchill, Gandhi, Dr. King, or Mother Theresa. As much as I've always loved

Willie Mays, I've never considered him a role model. Sports stars should never be considered role models. Any parent who abdicates his or her position as their child's role model to a sports star should have their parental privileges yanked. The best role models are people who are accessible and will always lead you in the right direction. Parents, teachers, community leaders, coaches, and successful coworkers are the kind of role models people should be looking for.

My role models were my parents; they're responsible for who I am more than anyone else I've ever known. From my mother, who had a big mouth, I learned to always speak up for myself, never take any crap, and to not be afraid to open your mouth and voice your opinion against things that aren't right.

From my father I learned about commitment and attitude. I learned that when you take a job, you commit to it every day. You show up every

(Continued)

(Continued)

day, do your job well, and don't complain. If you don't like the job, find another one. Otherwise find a way to make your job better or shut up.

My father never actually told me those things. Instead he showed me by how he lived his life every day. However, the most valuable lesson he ever taught me through his actions was: The best gift you can give your kids is your time. This is also a good idea for all you managers who need to develop that middle 80 percent.

What you want to do is give them a chance to interact more frequently with the top 10 percent. The middle 80 percent rarely get to talk to the top 10 percent because the top 10 percent are never around. They're busy! That's why they're the top 10 percent!

Amazingly, the *bottom* 10 percent have far more interaction with the middle group than the top

10 percent. Why? Because they always seem to be hanging around with nothing to do. That's what makes them the bottom 10 percent. They are the proverbial rotten apple that spoils the entire barrel. This, more than their total lack of production, is the biggest reason to get rid of them.

If they just kept to themselves and kept their mouths shut, it wouldn't be that terrible. But because they're always around, they're constantly chirping in the ear of the middle 80 percent (your most impressionable group). And what do you think the conversation is like between these two groups?

> Bottom 10 percent: "Hey, why are you working so hard? Let's get out of here and get a cup of coffee. You like working here? You do? Are you crazy? This place is awful. First chance I get, I'm out of here." (Sure, like employers are lined up waiting for this dope.) Bottom 10 percent: "What do you think of the boss?"
> Middle 80 percent: "I like him. He knows his stuff."

Bottom 10 percent: "Are you nuts!!?? I think he's an idiot. He must have a relative in upper management to get this job."

Again we come back to my theory that being a manager is a lot like being a parent. Don't you worry about the kind of people your kids are hanging out with? I know that when my daughter switched from hanging out with A student kids with strong outside interests to—well, let's just call them the bottom 10 percent—her behavior and grades suffered. It wasn't until college that she started to surround herself with top 10 percenters, and sure enough, she became one herself.

You should be worrying about who your people surround themselves with in the same way you worry about who your kids associate with. To help that middle 80 percent, give your top 10 percenters new responsibilities and challenges that will put them in contact with the middle group. Have them speak at your weekly meetings. Let them talk about their success and how they got to where they are and what they do to be successful. Let them mentor and train some younger, inexperienced people. Your top producers love and need new challenges. It keeps the job fresh and stops them from being bored. And the last thing you need is a bored top producer. Then you'll really have problems.

Chapter 8

Key #7—Help Your People Build Winning Streaks

There's nothing like a winning streak. If you don't believe me, try sitting on a losing streak for awhile; you'll see the difference. As a manager and leader it's up to you to help your people create and build winning streaks. In other words, set them up to succeed, not fail, on a daily basis. The best way to do that is to maximize a person's strengths and minimize their weaknesses.

A good way to start is to find what I call each person's level. In other words, what they are capable of doing, what they are not capable of doing,

97

Help Your People Build Winning Streaks

and how much they can handle and still feel good about what they've done and not get frustrated.

If you're not sure of what kind of work a person is capable of doing, start them off with easy tasks, tasks they're 100 percent certain to succeed at. As they master these easy tasks, start increasing the degree of difficulty a little bit at a time. Fairly soon you'll see what their comfort level is and, instead of forcing them to bust through it, you can get them to expand it a little bit at a time.

Leadership Tip: Don't Break Them Out of Their Comfort Zone—Expand Their Comfort Zone

Everyone's comfort zone is different. But like anything else in life, it doesn't matter what your comfort zone is. All that matters is that you know what it is, because only then can you figure out what you need to do to get beyond it.

As a manager you might have people operating in a comfort zone where their production is woefully short of what you need out of them. The problem is that your chances of getting them from where they are to where they need to be, and quickly, are anywhere from slim to none.

In order to get people to bust out of their comfort zones, you need to get them to do things they're not used to doing, will probably dislike, and are convinced they can't do.

I think the best way to illustrate this is to use a sales example, since sales results are quantifiable.

The easiest way to make sure your sales force wins on a daily basis is to give them activity goals along with their sales goals. Most salespeople don't have to close a sale on a daily basis in order to be successful, yet on those days when they don't close a sale, they feel like they failed.

If, along with their sales goals, they had a daily activity goal, they'd never fail. The only

(Continued)

Help Your People Build Winning Streaks

part of the sales process that is 100 percent within a salesperson's control is the actual generation of activity. You need someone else to say yes to an appointment or to close a sale, but the act of knocking on doors or making prospecting phone calls is totally the salesperson's responsibility. So if your people aren't hitting their activity goals on a daily basis, they're just not trying.

Now let's get to the part about expanding the salesperson's comfort zone rather than busting out of it.

Let's say one of your salespeople has a daily activity goal of 20 prospecting calls a day, but in reality he or she is only generating three calls a day. You could demand he start making 20 calls a day and he just might, for a while. But, since sales is mostly about rejection, you're asking that salesperson to get rejected about 80 more times per week than he's used to (17 more calls a day × 5 days = 85 more calls a week.

Maybe five people say yes to an appointment or one or two buy). Chances are he'll crack under the strain, dread coming to work every day, and eventually revert back to his old habits, which will probably lead to you firing him sometime.

But instead of asking your salespeople to bust out of their comfort zones and eventually give up in frustration, why not just ask them to expand their comfort zones by making one more call a day every day for a month. After the month is up, ask them to add on another call a day during the next month, and so on.

They might not reach an optimum activity goal immediately, but by doing it gradually and on an everyday consistent basis, they have a great chance of getting there. And by reaching their goal every day, they're building the confidence that comes with winning streaks.

Plus, let's say you have a sales force of 10 people. If each one made one extra call a day

(Continued)

Help Your People Build Winning Streaks

(*Continued*)

over and above what they're averaging, that's 10 extra calls a day, 50 extra calls a week, and at least 200 extra calls that first month. By the second month it's 400 extra calls over what they've been doing, 600 by the third month, and we're now up to 1,200 extra calls just by asking people to slightly expand their comfort zone. Can you imagine how many extra sales your people will close in the next three months from those 1,200 extra calls?

The key is: Small changes executed on a consistent everyday basis will always yield great results.

I think the story that best exemplifies the management practice of helping your people build winning streaks took place in North Africa in 1943 during World War II.

At that point in time, Field Marshall Erwin Rommel, the German Tank Commander, had just finished blitzing his way across North Africa. He left behind, in his wake, two badly beaten and demoralized armies: the American and the British.

These soldiers were so beaten they no longer had any sense of self-worth or self-esteem. Their uniforms were filthy and their camps were filthy.

Into this mess stepped two great leaders. General George Patton took command of the American troops in North Africa, and Field Marshall Bernard Montgomery assumed command of the British troops.

I don't know whether you know anything about Patton and Montgomery, but I can tell you they were as different as night and day. On top of that, they didn't particularly like each other. Montgomery thought Patton was an out-of-control American cowboy, and Patton thought Montgomery was a wuss.

However, as different as they were, they both faced the same problem: What was the long-term ultimate goal? Win the war, of course. But do you really think you could take troops in this condition and win a war? Patton and Montgomery knew they first needed some short-term goals.

Help Your People Build Winning Streaks

One was to get the troops to believe they could win the war. Another, even shorter-term goal, was to get them to believe they could do anything. Amazingly, Patton and Montgomery collaborated on the same solution.

All they asked was that each soldier do three things every day:

1. Wear a clean uniform.
2. Do 20 push-ups.
3. Run one mile.

Now that doesn't seem like much, but what did these two great leaders know? They knew they first had to build the confidence of the men and get them to reach their goals, and when you are achieving your goals on a continuous daily basis, your confidence starts to skyrocket. That's what happened.

As the troops became more and more confident, Patton and Montgomery gradually increased the difficulty of the tasks. Eventually, they built a lean, mean fighting machine. And for those of you who don't know how it ended: We won.

Chapter 9

Key #8—Stop Touching Everything

When I was 24 years old, I was promoted to the position of sales manager for one reason: I was a really good salesman, which is probably the worst reason to make someone a sales manager.

Most top salespeople just want to be left alone to do their job. Unfortunately, as a sales manager, being left alone is not an option. In addition, your team will include salespeople whose ability and production range from superstar to solid producer to mediocre to downright awful. Top salespeople who become sales manager very often have a tough time understanding why all salespeople don't have the same drive, ability, and level of production they have.

I was your typical top producing salesperson turned sales manager, and I was absolutely awful at the job. I had no patience for anyone whose production did not approach mine. But worst of all, I had a horrible need to be involved in everyone's business and every decision, no matter how small.

I was convinced I could do everybody else's job better than they could, which might have been true if I wasn't trying to do them all at the same time. It was a disaster.

The owner of the company called me in for a talk. He was a very smart guy and a shrewd businessman. He also had a habit of always talking in parables in order to get his point across. It was my turn to hear the parable of the day.

He told me a story about himself that occurred when he was my age. He was working for his father, who owned numerous businesses in and around New York City. The company where he worked at the time (the 1950s) distributed paper bags to independent bakeries throughout the city. He was the dispatcher, in charge of making sure all the delivery trucks got out on time and deliveries were completed in a timely and efficient manner.

One morning, as he told me, he had an argument with one of the drivers and fired him on the spot. To make sure the driver's deliveries were made, he drove the truck himself. That night at dinner his father asked him how it went that day. He replied, "Not bad, Dad. All went well except I had a problem with John [not real name] and had to fire him. But don't worry, I drove his route and got all his deliveries done."

His father looked at him and said, "Hey, stupid, how much do I pay the drivers?" He replied, "About $40 a week, Pop." (Remember, it's the 1950s.) His father then asked, "How much do I pay you?" "Two hundred dollars a week," he replied. Then his father said, "Why do I need a $200-a-week dispatcher driving a $40-a-week delivery truck?"

Stop Touching Everything

Moral of the story: *Stop touching everything*! You hired your people; let them do their jobs. If you don't think they can do it, show them how to do it better. If you find their hiring was a mistake, get rid of them; otherwise, get the hell out of the way.

I know you think you can do everyone else's job better than they can, but believe me, you can't. But even if by the slightest chance you could, why should you be paid a manager's salary for doing, let's say, an assistant's job?

Learn to let go. Trust your people. Let them develop their talents. It's going to make your job a lot easier.

Leadership Tip: Don't Be Afraid to Fire Someone

Let me start this by saying that I believe firing someone is a last resort. Your biggest responsibility, as a manager/leader, is to develop the talents and abilities of your people and to put them in situations where they have a great chance to succeed. But sometimes it just doesn't work out. You chose the wrong person, it turns out they weren't right for the job, or maybe they just couldn't cut it.

Stuff happens, and instead of hoping and praying the situation will get better, or spending an inordinate amount of time trying to salvage it, cut your losses. There's an old saying in the retail business, "Your first markdown is your best markdown."

How to fire someone is the one good thing I learned from Sal. The first time I needed to do it, I just couldn't. I didn't have the stomach for it. But then Sal sat me down and explained it to me in very simple terms. He said, "If someone is not doing their job it not only affects them, it affects you too, since you're judged on your team's performance as a whole. If this one person continues to drag your overall numbers down, not only will he be gone, but so will you."

(Continued)

Stop Touching Everything

(*Continued*)

Once he put it like that I had no problem pulling the trigger and haven't had one since. To this day I have never fired anyone who didn't deserve to be fired.

Chapter 10

Key #9—Help People Understand the Importance of Their Jobs

I'm Starting This Chapter with a Rant:

I *hate* it when I hear someone say, "I'm only the receptionist here." Or, "I'm only the assistant." I don't care what their position or job description is. Everyone in an organization is important, if not critical, to the success of that organization. Don't believe me; think about this: In many companies the only person who speaks to every single client is the receptionist! If you don't think

(Continued)

Help People Understand the Importance of Their Jobs

that can make an impact in either a positive or negative way, you're fooling yourself.

One thing successful companies understand better than anyone else is: Everybody sells! Just because you're not *in* sales, referred to as a salesperson, or responsible for bringing in business, doesn't mean you're not responsible for keeping what you already have and helping it grow.

Anyone working in a company, who has even the most indirect contact with clients, sells, because the attitudes and perceptions that clients form of a company come only from the people they deal with.

An installation crew, for example, although they didn't sell the equipment, can certainly impact the buying experience for the client in either a positive or negative way. Customer service is selling. If you don't believe it, try delivering lousy service and see how many clients you lose.

Every client interaction is an opportunity to make or break a client relationship.

The company I worked for in the New York City garment district had the world's meanest, nastiest head bookkeeper. I guarantee, if this woman ever smiled, her face would have broken in half. Once she actually returned a check, a perfectly good check, to a client, because it arrived with seven cents postage due. Needless to say, we lost the client.

It didn't matter to the client that, out of roughly 120 people who worked for the company, everyone was a very nice person except Sal. We lost that client because of one nasty, stupid jerk. That may not seem fair, but in reality it is, because at that moment the one nasty jerk was representing all 120 of us who worked for the company. People don't buy from companies or from buildings. People buy from other people, and the attitudes and perceptions that clients and prospects form of your

(*Continued*)

Help People Understand the Importance of Their Jobs

(*Continued*)

company will come only from the people they deal with.

So whether you manage salespeople, customer service reps, the IT department, installation technicians, clerical staff, or the accounting department, you're in sales, because every time one of your people interacts with a client, that person represents everyone in your company, and at that moment is the face of the company. Everybody sells! Everybody's job is important to the overall success of the company.

Do you know whose fault it is if your people don't understand the importance of their jobs and how it affects the company as a whole? It's *your* fault! How are they supposed to know how important they are in the larger scheme of things if you don't tell them? Don't assume they know.

Here's a good rule of thumb: Never assume! My philosophy is: The only time I'm sure that someone else knows exactly what I want is when I tell them.

When I worked for that small consulting firm in New York City we had a client who was a defense contractor. They manufactured bomb holders for NATO fighter jets. They brought us in because they had a quality control problem, and a quality control problem with bomb holders is serious stuff.

It seems the holders were holding the bombs either too loose or too tight. If too loose, the bombs would release prematurely and hit the wrong target. If too tight, the bombs wouldn't release and the wind current would push the bomb back up into the plane—not a good situation for the pilot.

Turns out the problem was a screw that needed to be turned one-quarter of a turn. An eighth of a turn and it's too loose; half a turn and it's too tight. These screws were being installed manually on an assembly line. You could blame the workers for sloppy work but, as it happens, nobody in management had ever told the workers why it was critical that each screw be turned exactly one-quarter of a turn.

These workers had no idea that what seemed to be an unimportant, mindless job had a major

Help People Understand the Importance of Their Jobs

impact on the overall quality of the product. When they found out, their attitude changed, and why wouldn't it?—for the first time ever they were being told they were important. They took far more pride in their work, and naturally the quality of their work improved tremendously.

You need to sit down with each one of your people separately and make sure they know the importance of their job and how it impacts the big picture. You never want to hear someone who works for you say, "I'm only a _____," because no matter how big or small the link in a chain is, they all need to be connected.

The people you manage are also your customers. They are the link between you and the external customers who drive your company. The attitude you take toward your people is the attitude they will deliver to the external customers, because remember—people don't buy from companies, people buy from other people, and the attitudes and perceptions your external customers form of your company will come only from the internal people they deal with.

Index

127

Index